Dance

I0867784

Hip-Hop Dance

By Trudy Becker

level 2 little blue readers

www.littlebluehousebooks.com

Copyright © 2024 by Little Blue House, Mendota Heights, MN 55120. All rights reserved. No part of this book may be reproduced or utilized in any form or by any means without written permission from the publisher.

Little Blue House is distributed by North Star Editions:
sales@northstareditions.com | 888-417-0195

Produced for Little Blue House by Red Line Editorial.

Photographs ©: iStockphoto, cover, 4, 7, 9, 13, 16, 19, 21, 24 (top left), 24 (top right), 24 (bottom right); Shutterstock Images, 10, 14–15, 23, 24 (bottom left)

Library of Congress Control Number: 2022919919

ISBN
978-1-64619-830-6 (hardcover)
978-1-64619-859-7 (paperback)
978-1-64619-914-3 (ebook pdf)
978-1-64619-888-7 (hosted ebook)

Printed in the United States of America
Mankato, MN
082023

About the Author

Trudy Becker lives in Minneapolis, Minnesota. She likes exploring new places and loves anything involving books.

Table of Contents

Spin and Turn

One kid dances in the middle of a crowd.
He spins and turns.
He balances on his hands and makes a shape in the air.

A girl listens to the music and dances.
All of her moves have high energy.
She moves her feet quickly.

A group dances together. The kids do the same moves but use their own style. They are dancing hip-hop.

All About It

Hip-hop dance is part of a group of art forms called hip-hop.

It is part of Black culture and started in New York City.

Break dancing is part of hip-hop dance. Dancers make shapes with their bodies. They need good balance and fast feet.

Hip-hop dance uses simple moves too. People can repeat them. They can use these moves when listening to hip-hop music.

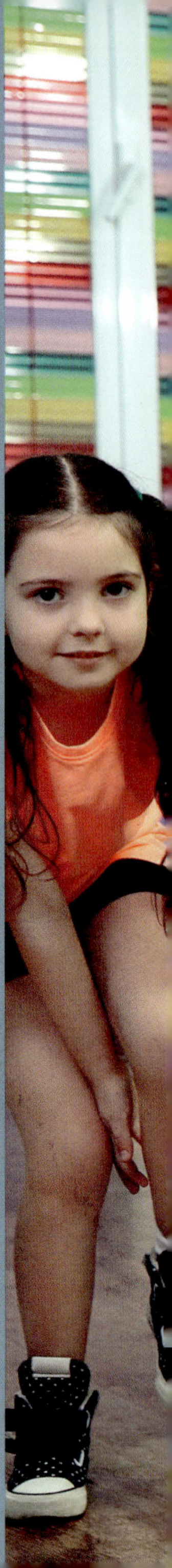

Learning How

Some people learn hip-hop dance with their friends. Some take lessons. They perform on stages or streets.

Hip-hop dancers practice their moves.

The moves should look amazing and show their feelings.

ANCE SCHOOL

Hip-hop dancers can wear different things. Many wear loose clothes. They might wear hats. The clothing and dances both show their style.

Before performing,
dancers get ready.
They loosen up.
They check the music.
It is time for
hip-hop dance!

Glossary

balance

hat

crowd

lesson

Index